EVERYDAY GUIDES
MADE EASY

MICROSOFT
WINDOWS
BASICS

JAMES STABLES

**FLAME TREE
PUBLISHING**

CONTENTS

SERIES FOREWORD

Windows, which launched in 1985, began as a way to navigate PCs without having to resort to command prompts, and although early versions might look clunky by today's standards, the concept of navigating a computer through 'windows' rather than through hard-to-remember commands immediately caught on. Millions of installs later, Windows is the most popular computer operating system on the planet, with more than 1.25 billion PCs running a version of Windows today.

To compliment Windows in the business space, Microsoft developed Microsoft Office back in 1990, and without Office programs like Word, Excel and PowerPoint our world would look very different today.

This *Microsoft Windows Basics* guide is designed to take you from zero to hero without any of the pain, but fear not, we won't bamboozle you with jargon. We'll start with the basics of this feature-rich software, progressing through to advanced functions and finally troubleshooting. Each chapter has a number of Hot Tips that'll ensure you're on the very cutting edge without lifting a finger.

This step-by-step guide is written by an acknowledged expert on Windows, so you can be sure of the best advice, and it is suitable for anyone from the complete beginner through to advanced users who would like a refresher. You'll find this guide an excellent reference volume on all Microsoft Windows has to offer, and it will grace your bookcase for years to come.

Mark Mayne
Editor of T3.com

INTRODUCTION

This guide tells you everything you need to know to get started with Windows. From the very basics to expert tools, *Microsoft Windows Basics* has it all.

WINDOWS 8 OR WINDOWS 8.1?

Windows 8.1 is the 2013 update to Microsoft's Windows 8, which was released in 2012. This book has been written specifically for the Home version of Windows 8.1 and covers all the new features that the update has brought with it. If you are running Windows 8, or even Windows 7, don't fear, you can still use this guide.

Above: Don't despair! This book will help you get the most out of Windows.

IN-DEPTH CHAPTERS

We take you from the basics of the system to some of its best and most hidden features, with screenshots taken along the way. You'll discover that Microsoft Windows is the perfect operating system, whether you're an absolute beginner or a seasoned IT professional.

STEP-BY-STEP GUIDES

Each section of this guide features easy-to-follow step-by-step guides which walk you through every aspect of Windows' numerous features. *Microsoft Windows Basics* offers clear and concise explanations for every part of the operating system.

Above: All the screenshots in this book have been chosen to highlight or further illustrate what is being said in the text.

Hot Tips

Look out for hot tips to get even more out of your Windows experience: from quick shortcuts to hacks for power users.

INTRODUCING WINDOWS

WELCOME TO WINDOWS

Windows runs on nearly all PCs sold around the world, and is by far the most popular operating system on the planet.

WHAT IS WINDOWS 8.1?

Windows 8.1 is the latest edition of the world's most popular PC operating system from Microsoft. It has a Modern User Interface – and its focus is on apps and a touch-friendly interface.

WHAT'S NEW IN WINDOWS 8.1?

After the initial release of Windows 8 came an update which fixed some issues and complaints with the original operating system. This added a whole new set of features and some minor usability tweaks. Windows 8.1 is a free update to any existing users.

Windows 8.1 Features

- Apps from the Windows Store

- New Start screen with live updates

- Built-in web storage

- Familiar desktop area

- Works with a mouse and keyboard

- Full support and compatibility with programs

Above: One of the great new features Windows 8.1 comes with is a revamped Start screen with the addition of live updates.

- Works with nearly all hardware

- Built for touch PCs and tablets

- Built-in web search

- Faster boot times

- Better performance on the same hardware

Above: The Windows 8.1 Start screen is your gateway to a whole new Windows experience.

Windows 8.1 Features

Windows 8.1 packs in a host of updates. Changes include:

- The Start button

- Boot to the desktop first

- Support for 3D printing

- Updates to all Windows apps

- Add photos to the lock screen

- Support for four apps on screen at once and resizing windows to any dimension

- Search within apps

- Fingerprint security to protect files

Hot Tip

If you're still on Windows 8, find your free upgrade to Windows 8.1 in the Windows Store – just tap on the app to download and install.

Above: Windows 8.1 brings back the familiar Start button in the lower-left corner of your screen.

WINDOWS TERMINOLOGY EXPLAINED

Navigating Windows can be challenging for the uninitiated, but fear not. Here's some of the jargon explained to get you started.

Lock Screen
The Windows 8.1 welcome screen – you will be asked to enter your password here if using a Microsoft account.

Start Screen
This is the main screen in Windows 8.1. All your apps are here.

Desktop
The desktop is the classic Windows look. Icons for your programs appear here.

Above: Pictured is the interactive Start screen, from which all your files, apps and other services are accessed.

Start Button
The Windows icon at the bottom-left of the desktop screen. Tap or click to return to the Start screen.

Window
Everything you do is contained within a window, whether you're playing a game

Above: A pro of snap view is that two apps can be open on the same screen, allowing you to work on both at once.

or looking at files on a USB stick. You can open, close, hide and switch between windows at will.

Window Snapping

In Windows 8.1, you can snap windows to either side of the screen, so apps and folders can be used side-by-side.

Taskbar

The bar along the bottom of the desktop is called the taskbar. Hovering over an icon will open a preview of that task.

Title Bar

At the top of a window is a long bar. This is the title bar, and you can click this to drag the window around.

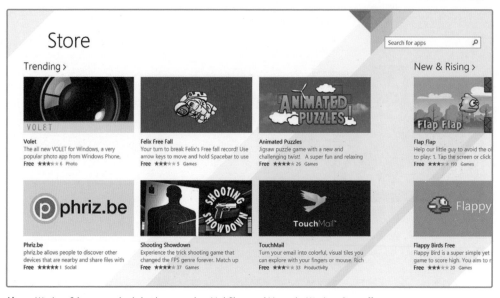

Above: Windows 8.1 comes preloaded with apps, such as Mail, Photo and Music; the Windows Store offers many more, in categories including Entertainment, Travel and Education.

Toolbar
The toolbar will be found under the title bar, but not in the main window itself.

Apps
Apps are the programs that open when you click items on the Start screen. You can download more apps in the Windows Store and most of them are free.

Icons
These are small pictures that represent a link to a program or app. You will see icons on the desktop and taskbar.

Tile
The icon on the Start screen that launches apps in Windows 8.1.

Charms

Quick links to sharing, devices, settings and the search facility are known as 'charms' and are shown on the right-hand side of the screen.

Trackpad

The touch-sensitive pad found on laptops, for controlling the cursor.

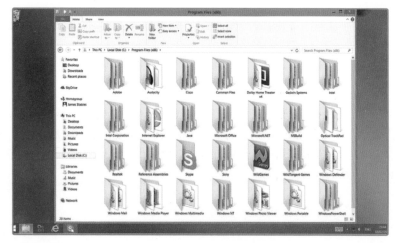

Above: Organize your data by storing it in files and folders: it's then easy to find.

Cursor

The pointer that you move around the screen.

File

Any document, image, song or movie will be stored as a single element called a file.

Folder

This is the area in which files are stored.

Left-Click

A single left-click on your mouse will select an item, while double-clicking will open it. You can also left-click by tapping a touch screen or the main part of the trackpad.

Right-Click

Right-clicking can be done by clicking files or within folders or on the desktop. Right-clicking on touch screens is done by tapping and then holding for three seconds.

WHAT CAN I DO WITH WINDOWS 8.1?

From getting online for the first time to running a business, Windows is used around the world by every imaginable type of user. Its open and compatible nature means you can do almost anything with a Windows PC.

SURF THE WEB

Once connected you can use Internet Explorer to surf the web. Using the News, Sports, Email and other apps on the Start screen will bring the web to you.

Above: Windows 8.1 has many apps that make it easy to access the internet in a variety of ways.

SEND EMAIL

You can find a Mail application on the Start screen. You can download alternatives from the Windows Store or the web.

ENJOY YOUR PHOTOS

Windows 8.1 brings all your photos together in one place. As it is designed for touch screens, it's like having your own photo album to browse.

LISTEN TO MUSIC

Above: The Photo app allows you to edit your photos, using the options shown here.

The Xbox Music app lets you search and listen to music from the internet, even if you haven't bought it. If you have downloaded music, Windows Media Player can find your files, organize and play them.

WATCH TV AND MOVIES

The Xbox Video service has top movies which can be rented or bought; it will also play any files you already own.

PLAY GAMES

Choose from simple puzzle games to more immersive 3D titles. If you have an Xbox, you can add your Xbox Live account to the games app.

Hot Tip

Love games? Head to the Windows Store, where you'll find hundreds of them, many of which are free to download.

Above: The People app shows all of your friends' latest updates and posts.

Above: With the Skype app, it's easy to keep in touch with friends or family who are far away.

STAY IN TOUCH WITH FRIENDS

Windows 8.1 has 'baked-in' Facebook and Twitter integration and dedicated apps, plus a People app, where contacts can be pulled in from across different services.

VIDEO CHAT

Most Windows PCs have built-in cameras and official support for Skype in Windows 8.1.

CREATE DOCUMENTS

Microsoft Office has always been the staple of PC users, but if you don't fancy forking out for Office, there are other free options:

- Microsoft OneDrive
- OpenOffice
- Google Drive

STAY SAFE ONLINE

User Account Control prevents any installation without your explicit permission, and Windows Defender, a built-in utility that's been revamped in Windows 8.1, offers you out-of-the-box protection.

INTRODUCING THE START SCREEN

Windows 8.1's new look can open up a whole new computing experience. Let us guide you around the Start screen.

THE WINDOWS 8.1 START SCREEN

1. **Charm bar**: Swipe in from the right on a touch-screen device, moving your mouse to the bottom right-hand corner of the screen or hitting Win + C on the keyboard.

2. **Search**: The first element on the Charm bar is Search. This charm brings up a box in which you can type what you're looking for.

3. **Share**: Using the Share charm will give you options for sending content to others.

4. **Start**: Hit this charm to be returned to the Start screen in double-quick fashion.

5. **Devices**: This charm enables you to interact with devices in one handy place.

6. **Settings**: You get quick links to customizations or you can hit PC Settings in the bottom-right corner to bring up a settings menu.

7. **Time and date**: The time and date dominates a black panel, which can be accessed with a swipe from the right or by placing the mouse in the bottom right-hand corner.

Hot Tip

Pinch in on the screen if using a touch screen or use the Windows key + the minus key to reduce the size of Start-screen tiles.

8 **Battery level**: If using a laptop or tablet device, you can see the battery level or progress of charging.

9 **Wireless**: If you're connected to a wireless network, you'll get an icon with some bars.

10 **Options bar**: By swiping up from the bottom, or pressing the Start menu, you can bring up the Options bar.

11 **User**: Your username and display picture will be shown in the top-right of the Start screen.

12 Apps: Apps will be displayed on the Start screen, and you can drag the tiles around as desired.

13 Desktop: For the Windows desktop, there's a tile on the Start screen.

14 Live tiles: Tiles are icons for apps.

15 Background theme: Change colour using the Settings charm.

Hot Tip

Swipe down, or click the down arrow on the Start screen, to get a full list of the installed apps in Windows 8.1. You can then choose what to have on your main screen, keeping it tidy and organized just how you want.

Above: When you install a new app from the Windows Store, it'll appear in the Apps view.

INTRODUCING THE DESKTOP

The addition of the Start screen might dominate the Windows 8.1 experience, but the old desktop is only one click or tap away.

THE WINDOWS 8.1 DESKTOP

1. **Desktop**: The wide open space for all your windows, files and folders.

2. **Background**: A customizable background, which, unlike the Start screen, can be changed to anything you want.

3. **Icons**: Any file, folder or shortcut to a program can be laid out as you need it.

4. **Taskbar**: The bar running along the bottom is the taskbar.

5. **Pinned programs**: Programs can be pinned to the taskbar to be launched quickly. Drag to the bar to keep it there and right-click to remove it.

6. **Lists**: When an item is pinned to the taskbar, it can benefit from Jump Lists. Right-click any item to access the list.

7. **On-screen keyboard**: Summon a keyboard by pressing the icon on the taskbar.

8. **Time and date**: Time and date is displayed on the right-hand side of the taskbar. Click it to make adjustments.

9. **Running tasks**: You can see all background apps and tasks that are running in the notification area, on the right of the taskbar.

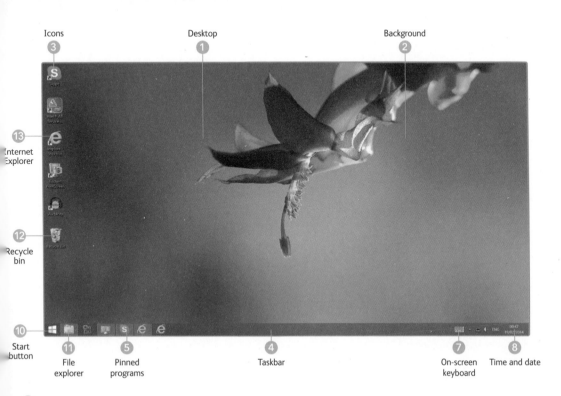

Icons

Desktop

Background

Internet
Explorer

Recycle
bin

Start
button

File
explorer

Pinned
programs

Taskbar

On-screen
keyboard

Time and date

10 **Start button**: Another way to get back to the Start screen.

11 **File Explorer**: This icon will open a new window to access traditional folders.

12 **Recycle bin**: To delete items, just drag to the bin.

13 **Internet Explorer**: The gateway to the internet.

14 **Return To Desktop**: There's an invisible hotspot at the bottom-right, which will minimize all windows to reveal the desktop.

15 **Charm bar**: From the traditional desktop, you can still access the Charm bar.

WINDOWS 8.1 MADE EASIER

One thing is guaranteed in Windows 8.1, and that's that every option and feature has a hidden shortcut for getting it done more quickly and easily.

JUMP LISTS

Using the Windows 8.1 desktop is a great way to get more done, and the Jump List feature epitomizes how powerful this area of Windows can be.

Accessing Jump Lists

1. Drag your favourite Windows 8.1 programs to your desktop taskbar, or right-click (or long-press) items from the Windows Start screen and choose Pin to Taskbar.

2. To access the Jump Lists, right-click a taskbar item. Touch screen users can long-press on the icon.

3. Each Jump List is split into three items: Frequent, Tasks and general items.

USE THE ON-SCREEN KEYBOARD

One of the huge improvements in Windows 8.1 is its focus on touch screens. On a Windows tablet, the on-screen keyboard will be a huge part of your experience.

Frequent
- 🏠 Welcome to the Sony VAIO portal
- Ⓜ MSN
- Ⓢ Skype sign in - Sign in to your Sk...
- ⊞ Update to Windows 8.1: FAQ - M...
- W Microsoft Windows - Wikipedia, ...

Tasks
- Start InPrivate Browsing
- Open new tab

- 🌐 Internet Explorer
- Unpin this program from taskbar
- ❌ Close all windows

Right: Master Jump Lists, and everything you need will be just a click away.

Bring Up The Keyboard

The on-screen keyboard will appear when Windows thinks you want to input text and detects there's not a physical one attached. You can also summon the keyboard using the icon on the taskbar.

Hot Tip

Just like older versions of Windows, you can press Alt +F4 to shut down apps quickly and easily.

MAKE YOUR PC EASIER TO USE

If you find using a PC difficult, Windows 8.1 is packed with customizations and tools to make your life easier.

Above: Windows' on-screen keyboard is intuitive, and gives easy access to numbers and common symbols.

Make Your Screen Easier To See

1. Head to the Search charm, choosing PC Settings and then Ease of Access.

2. Choose Magnifier from the list.

3. In the left-hand pane, choose High contrast.

Make Text Larger

1. Swipe in from the right edge of the screen, then choose Settings.

2. Tap or click PC and devices and then tap or click Display.

3. Look for the More options heading. Under Change the size of apps, make sure it's set to the largest option.

Make Using The Mouse Easier

1. Return to the Ease of Access menu and choose Mouse from the list of options.

2. From here, you can change the colour and size of mouse pointers to make things easier. The cursor will change on screen as soon as you select an option, so you can try it on for size.

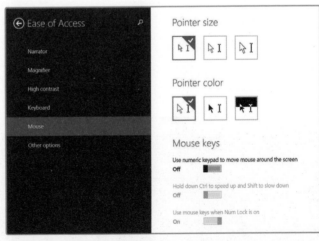

Above: The Ease of Access/Mouse menu lists many options, as shown here, so it's simple to find one that works for you.

3. Once you're done, just return to the home screen.

4. You can turn on mouse keys in the Ease of Access menu, enabling the arrow keys on your keyboard to move the pointer instead.

Simplify Using The Keyboard

1. Return to the Ease of Access menu and choose Keyboard.

2. If you struggle with complex keyboard shortcuts, you can turn on Sticky Keys. This means you can press key combos concurrently, but not simultaneously, to launch commands.

3. Toggle Keys alert you if you press the Caps Lock, Num Lock or Scroll Lock keys.

4. When you turn on Filter Keys, Windows ignores it when you press the same key rapidly or when you press keys for several seconds unintentionally.

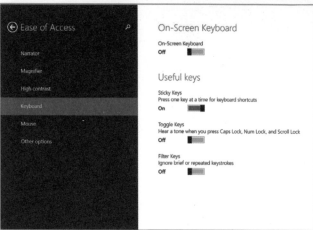

Above: The Ease of Access/Keyboard settings are invaluable for users who struggle to press more than one key at a time.

GETTING STARTED

SETTING UP WINDOWS 8.1

It's quick to get started with Windows 8.1, but things aren't as simple as the old days: here we show you how to install the new OS and get started.

INSTALL WINDOWS 8.1

Most people's first experience with Windows 8.1 will be via a new PC; however, you can buy the OS on disk and install it. See below:

1. Turn PC on to start Windows, insert DVD or USB flash drive, then restart and press any key to boot.

2. On the Install Windows page, enter your language and other preferences, then tap or click Next, then Install Windows. On the Enter the product key to activate Windows page, enter your product key.

3. You'll then be asked to click the partition that you want. Most systems will have a C: drive; however, if dual-booting, choose an empty partition rather than the C: drive.

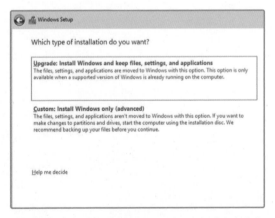

Personalize Windows

First, Windows 8.1 will ask you to choose the colour for your experience and set-up. You'll then be asked to name your PC. Connect your Wi-Fi by choosing it from the list.

Above: Before upgrading to Windows 8.1, make sure you have backed up your files.

Express Setup

You'll now see the Settings menu. You can use custom settings or express. Most users will be fine with the standard express settings.

YOUR MICROSOFT ACCOUNT

Windows 8.1 is designed to be paired with an email address, to link your PC with your online life. Read on to find out how to set up your Windows ID.

Setting Up A Microsoft Account

1. Type your email address into the box provided. If you haven't got one already, or if you don't have access to the account, click Sign up for a new email address in the list at the bottom.

2. If you choose to create a new email address, you'll be asked for a small amount of personal information and to choose what email address you want.

3. You can choose the prefix – the name before the @ symbol – select from outlook.com, hotmail.com or live.com, and choose a password before clicking or tapping Next.

Hot Tip

Using your email as a Microsoft account doesn't affect the use of the original service, so you won't notice any changes to your Gmail, for example. What's more, if you choose to use a different password for Windows 8.1 – which is advised for basic security – your old one will remain the same.

Above: You can use any existing email address for your Microsoft account – Outlook.com, Gmail, or Yahoo!, for example.

4. You'll now be directed to the Windows Start screen. When you log in to your PC in future, you'll need to use the password for your account, so don't forget it.

CHOOSE YOUR BROWSER

Your internet browser is the program that enables you to browse the web, and lets you enter the web address and displays the website you navigate to.

Browser choices include:

○ **Internet Explorer**

○ **Google Chrome**

○ **Firefox**

Hot Tip

Windows 8.1 enables you to make special accounts for children. When creating a new account, choose Add a child's account from the list. You can also opt to set up without an email address.

SET UP USER ACCOUNTS

Set Up A New User

To start adding family members, head to the Start screen and access the Setting charm by swiping from the right, or placing your mouse in the bottom right-hand corner. Choose PC Settings from the list and then choose Users. Click or tap Add a user.

ADMINISTRATOR ACCOUNTS

If you're looking to set up accounts for your family, but are worried about letting kids or other users have access to the advanced workings of your PC, you're in luck.

Above: Only the main account holder, or administrator, is able to make changes, such as installing new software.

Manage Your Users

You can change the status of any account, upgrading and downgrading it as you please. To make changes to accounts on your Windows 8.1 PC, choose Manage another account.

SET UP PARENTAL CONTROLS

Windows PCs are a great way for children to learn – and have fun – but using the internet and Windows 8.1 apps can lead to inquisitive minds stumbling across things they shouldn't. That's where parental controls come in. In Windows 8.1, these features are called Family Safety. You can access it by typing 'Family Safety' while the Start screen is open and choosing it from the Settings menu. Choose an account in the list and then tick On to apply Family Safety. Features include:

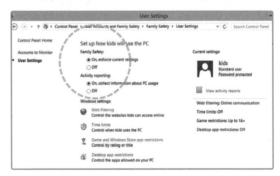

- **Activity Reporting**

- **Web Filtering**

- **Time Limits**

Above: If each child in your family has their own account, you can tailor the Family Safety measures according to their ages.

WINDOWS 8.1 SETTINGS

Windows 8.1 is one of the most customizable operating systems out there, and there's a host of settings at your fingertips.

MAKE WINDOWS WORK YOUR WAY

To access the PC Settings menu, open the Charms bar and choose Settings. Choose PC Settings. A new screen will appear with a host of options, which we'll talk you through now.

PC And Devices

Here, you can tweak the lock screen and monitor settings, Bluetooth, the mouse and trackpad, among other options.

Above: The options in the Settings panel allow you to personalize almost anything in Windows 8.1.

Accounts
Manage your account and change your profile picture, as well as quickly add new users.

Search And Apps
Here, you can tweak the results from the Search charm within Windows 8.1, as well as the way in which other Charms work. There are also settings for sharing, and you can see which apps are taking up the most room on your hard drive. Every app is listed with a simple slider, so you can choose whether alerts are on or off.

Privacy
This menu puts you in control of your information and data.

Network
The chief option for sharing is called HomeGroup and is accessible through the Network option in the PC Settings menu. Turn to our guide on page 84.

Time And Language
You can change time settings in this menu as well as world time-zone settings.

Ease Of Access
Putting your Start screen into high-contrast mode can make options easier to see.

Update and Recovery
Windows Update will notify you of any updates you have not yet installed.

> **Hot Tip**
>
> If you're hankering after more complex settings, press Win + X to launch a menu with quick links to **Network Connections, Computer Management and more.**

Above: Choose which network to connect to in the Network/Connections menu.

CUSTOMIZE WINDOWS 8.1

You can quickly make changes to the Start screen via the Settings charm, but to customize the desktop, just right-click on the desktop and choose Personalize.

GIVE WINDOWS YOUR OWN STAMP

While the Start screen is relatively plain in its design, the desktop is a place where you can really go to town.

Windows Themes

Click a theme to apply it and then click Save. You're not limited to the themes in the menu either. Click the link labelled Get more themes online and you can download new ones.

Above: The desktop is as good a place as any to start when it comes to personalizing your PC.

Above: Alert sound annoying you? Head to the Sounds option and change away!

Change Backgrounds

To make any picture your desktop background, click Desktop background and you'll get a view of your Pictures library. Choose any image. Alternatively right-click any image file and choose Set as desktop background.

Save Your Custom Theme

In Unsaved theme in the main Personalization window, click Save theme and give it a name.

Change Windows Colour

On the title bar choose any shade just by clicking Color at the bottom of the Personalize screen. Use the slider to change intensity.

Change Sounds

You can change those tones in the Sounds option, and even replace them with your own sounds, should you wish.

Set A Screensaver

Choose the screensaver from the list, and change options such as text or colour using the Settings box, and when you're done, click Apply.

Alter Desktop Icons

In Personalization, choose Change Desktop Icons, choose an item from the desktop, click Change Icon and then find one that suits.

Hot Tip

Played around with your icons too much? If you're sick of your new-look icons, just go back to the Change Desktop Icons menu and click the Restore Default button.

SET UP THE ESSENTIALS

Whether it's setting up your printers or overcoming bugbears with the system, we show you how to get the essentials sorted.

BOOT STRAIGHT TO THE WINDOWS DESKTOP

1. Go to the desktop, right-click (or press and hold) on the taskbar and choose Properties.

2. Click or press the Navigation tab.

3. Check When I sign in or close all apps on a screen, go to the desktop instead of Start. Touch or click OK.

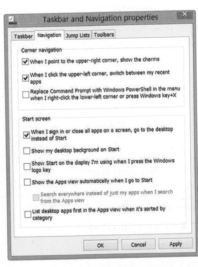

Above: Boot to desktop – useful for non-touch users – is new in Windows 8.1.

INSTALL A PRINTER

Windows 8.1 is compatible with most hardware and software, which makes setting up printers really easy.

Quick Start

To install your printer, just plug it in via a USB cable. Switch on, and wait for the hardware to be detected. You should get a notification that Windows has found an attached device.

Confirm The Install

Once Windows has found the drivers and installed them, you are ready to print. Go to an app, choose to print and you should see it listed.

TRANSFER FILES FROM A WINDOWS 7 PC

Windows Easy Transfer backs up all your files, which can then be uploaded into Windows 8.1.

Make The Switch

First, you'll need a USB storage device with plenty of room.

1. On your Windows 7 PC, go to the Start menu and type 'easy transfer' into the search box. Press Next and choose USB storage from the list.

2. Windows 7 will scan the PC for items you might want to back up. It puts these under the headings of User and Shared items.

Resurrect Your Files On Windows 8.1

1. Go to your Windows 8.1 PC and plug in your USB device.

2. Search for 'easy transfer' on the Start screen.

3. Click Next and you'll see 'Have you already used Windows Easy Transfer to save your files from another PC?' Choose Yes.

4. A box will open. Go to your storage device, which will be listed in the left-hand pane, and find the Windows Easy Transfer file.

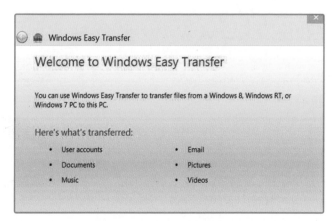

5. Press Open and you'll see a summary of the User and Shared files.

Above: Easy Transfer helps move documents in one process.

6. If your old PC had multiple user accounts and you have these set up on your new Windows 8.1 PC, click Advanced.

7. Press Transfer.

GESTURES AND SHORTCUTS

Windows 8.1 is full of shortcuts. Once you have mastered them you will have Windows 8.1's power at your fingertips.

MOUSE GESTURES

○ **Get back to the Start screen**: Point to the bottom-left corner and click it.

○ **Open the charms**: Point to the top-right or bottom-right corner to see charms.

○ **See all apps**: Click the down arrow in the bottom-left corner of the Start screen.

○ **Get to commands and context menus in an application**: Right-click within the application, then click the command you want. Alternatively, right-click an item to see the options specific to that item.

○ **Switch between open apps**: To switch to your most recently used application, point to the top-left corner. When the previous application appears, click the Preview window.

Above: When switching, try to direct the mouse's pointer up into the left-hand corner so it disappears.

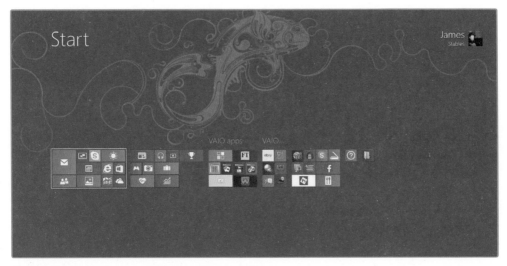

Above: By zooming out, you can see all the apps you have on your Start screen.

○ **Switch to a different app**: To switch to a different application, point to the top-left corner and then move down the edge. When the other applications appear, click the one you want.

○ **Open the desktop**: Go to the Start screen, then click the Desktop tile.

○ **Zoom in or out on Start**: Move your mouse to the bottom-right corner and press the Summary View icon to get an overview of every app tile, or press Ctrl + and scroll the mouse wheel to zoom out. Click anywhere to zoom back in.

○ **Arrange tiles**: Drag your application from the top of the screen and place it on the left or right side, then go to the Start screen and click another application.

○ **Close current application**: Point to the top edge of the screen, then drag the application to the bottom of the screen.

○ **Shut down your PC**: Point to the bottom-right corner. When the charms appear, move up, then click Settings. Click Power, then choose a shut-down option.

> ## Hot Tip
>
> In the taskbar Properties menu, you can turn off the hot corners, which show the charms and window-switching features. Click the Navigation tab and then untick the options at the top.

○ **Close open apps**: Point to the top-left corner and then move down the edge. Right-click the one you want, then click Close.

GENERAL WINDOWS SHORTCUTS

Above: Ctrl + Alt + Delete brings up the Task Manager, which shows you the programs currently running on your computer.

F1:	Help
Ctrl + Esc:	Open Start menu
Alt + Tab:	Switch between open programs
Alt + F4:	Quit program
Shift + Delete:	Delete item permanently
Ctrl + Alt + Delete:	Start up Task Manager
Windows key + L:	Lock the computer
Ctrl + C:	Copy selected text
Ctrl + X:	Cut the selected text
Ctrl + V:	Paste text in current location
Ctrl + Z:	Undo last action
Ctrl + B:	Make selected text bold
Ctrl + U:	Underline selected text
Ctrl + I:	Make selected text italic

WINDOWS 8.1 KEYBOARD SHORTCUTS

Windows logo key + start typing:	Search your PC
Ctrl + (+) or Ctrl + (-):	Zoom in or out of the Start screen
Windows key + C:	Open the charms
Windows key + F:	Open the Search charm to search files
Windows key + H:	Open the Share charm
Windows key + I:	Open the Settings charm
Windows key + K:	Open the Devices charm
Windows key + O:	Lock the screen orientation
Windows key + Q:	Open the Search charm to search everywhere or within an open app
Windows key + S:	Open the Search charm to search Windows and the web
Windows key + W:	Open the Search charm to search Settings
Windows key + Z:	Show the commands available in the application
Windows key + space-bar:	Switch input language and keyboard layout
Windows key + Ctrl + space-bar:	Change to a previously selected input
Windows key + Tab:	Cycle through recently used desktop applications
Windows key + Ctrl + Tab:	Cycle through recently used Windows 8.1 apps
Windows key + Shift + Tab:	Cycle through recently used applications (except desktop applications) in reverse order
Windows key + Left/Right key:	Snap an application to the left or right side of the screen.
Windows key + full stop (.):	Cycle through open applications
Esc:	Stop or exit the current task

TOUCH GESTURES

Select or Perform an Action
Just tap any item to launch it.

App-specific Commands
To get extra commands and options, swipe up from the bottom of the screen.

Get More Options
Press and hold on the screen for three seconds to see the context menu.

Scroll Through Windows
Place your finger on the screen and move it up, down, left or right to move the page.

Close an Application
Press and hold the screen at the top edge and then drag the window to the bottom to close it.

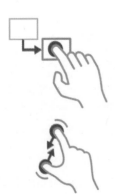

Drag and Move
Press and hold an item to select it and move your finger around the screen (still holding down) to reposition it.

Zoom In and Out
Pinch your fingers together on the screen to zoom in and separate them to zoom out.

Above: To arrange the windows side by side, drag their title bars to the required side of the screen.

Access the Charms Bar
Swipe your finger in from the right-hand edge to reveal the Charms bar.

Turn and Pivot Items
Hold two fingers on an item you want to rotate and twist them in a circular motion.

Switch Between Apps
To switch back to the last item you were working on, swipe your finger in from the left-hand side.

SECURE YOUR PC

It's easy to stay secure as there are tools built in to Windows 8.1 and even more freely available on the internet to help you stay safe.

WINDOWS DEFENDER

In the Windows 8.1 Start screen, just type 'defender' and then choose the program from the results. Windows Defender uses a traffic-light system. If the top bar is green and there's a tick on the computer screen graphic, then all is well. If there's another colour, there's work to do.

Check The Status

To see if Windows Defender is on and functioning properly, there are two status lines in the main screen. The first says Real-time protection, which should say 'On', and the second is Virus and spyware definitions, which should say 'Up to date'. If either of those two statuses says anything different, you'll need to take action.

Run A Scan

To run a scan of your PC, look at the right of the Windows Defender pane, where you'll see a box with scanning options.

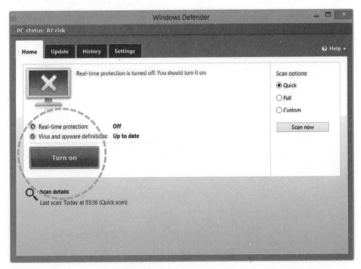

Above: Turn on Defender to protect your computer.

PROTECT YOUR PC WITH A SECURE LOG-IN

One of the biggest threats to your PC, aside from malware, is theft, and this is particularly important for people who use a Windows 8.1 laptop or tablet.

Stop Unauthorized Access To Your Files

Make sure you use a Microsoft ID. If you're not already using a Microsoft account, you can set it up by going to Settings in the Charms bar, Accounts and then Use a Microsoft account. Set a password and your PC will be secure.

Hot Tip

**Swapping numbers for similar letters is a great way to make your password secure.
Try swapping an @ symbol for an a and a 3 for an e.
Using upper-case letters also adds an extra level of security.**

Above: Once you have a Microsoft account, you can set up (and change) a password to prevent unauthorized access to your files.

Above: Confirm your picture and crop, then you will be asked to create three gestures on your picture, which will be the password.

Use A Picture Password

If you don't want to use a complex password to secure your PC, Windows 8.1 offers an alternative called Picture Password. To set it up:

1. Swipe in from the right edge of the screen, tap Settings, then tap Change PC settings, or if using a mouse, click Settings, then Change PC settings. Tap or click Accounts, and choose Sign-in options.

Hot Tip

It can be difficult to log in using a Picture Password, so use a range of gestures. It's much better to choose an image that has sentimental value, so you can set up points on the image that you'll remember.

2. Under Picture Password, tap or click Add. Click Choose picture to select a photo for your sign-in.

3. Draw three patterns on the screen. As you draw, the highlighted number on the left will change. You can draw a shape, a line or just tap the screen. When you've drawn all three, repeat. Press Finish and your Picture Password will be applied.

BACK UP WINDOWS

Disaster can strike at any time and, in seconds, whole digital lives can be erased due to hardware crashes, disk failures or, in rare cases, malware infections. It can happen to anyone, and it doesn't matter whether you have a budget system or an expensive Ultrabook, a Mac or a PC, new or old. Luckily, Windows 8.1 makes it easy to protect your files from digital disaster.

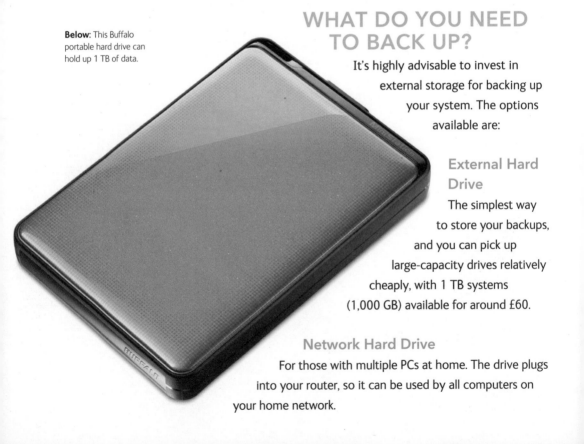

Below: This Buffalo portable hard drive can hold up 1 TB of data.

WHAT DO YOU NEED TO BACK UP?

It's highly advisable to invest in external storage for backing up your system. The options available are:

External Hard Drive

The simplest way to store your backups, and you can pick up large-capacity drives relatively cheaply, with 1 TB systems (1,000 GB) available for around £60.

Network Hard Drive

For those with multiple PCs at home. The drive plugs into your router, so it can be used by all computers on your home network.

Cloud Storage

Online storage, known as cloud storage, has grown hugely in the last few years, and with home broadband speeds improving, backing up your system over the internet is now a viable solution.

RAID

RAID uses two backup drives which mirror their data, effectively making a copy of a copy. It's rather tricky to set up, costly and not suitable for everyone.

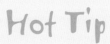

Hot Tip

File History is an extremely powerful backup tool and will make copies of your files to an external drive every 10 minutes if you choose. You can tweak the frequency in the Advanced menu.

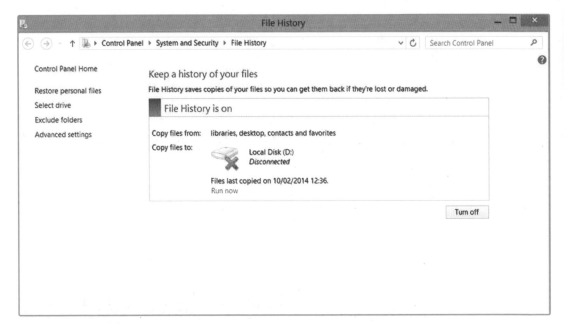

Above: Turn on File History in order to save a backup of all your files to an external hard drive.

WAYS TO BACK UP IN WINDOWS

There are many ways to back up your
Windows 8.1 system and keep your
files safe, with each method offering
slightly different benefits.

FILE HISTORY

File History is a new backup tool within
Windows 8.1, which makes it easy to
back up your system to whichever
media you choose.

Start Backups In File History

When you plug in a drive for the first time, Windows 8.1 will ask if you want to configure the drive for use with File History – a backup tool. Tap or click the option, and opt to switch on File History.

USE SYSTEM IMAGE BACKUP

The System Image feature enables you to take a snapshot of your entire system and save it to an external drive. If the worst were to happen, you could resurrect this image on a new system and have everything back the way it was before. To restore, head to the Recovery menu, go to Advanced Startup and hit the Troubleshoot option. Choose Advanced options, then System Image Recovery.

SYSTEM RESTORE

While you use your PC, Windows 8.1 automatically takes snapshots of your system to use as a Restore Point. If you suffer a PC crash, you can go back to a point when your PC worked well, though your files won't be up to date.

Above: Choose where to store your system backup (System Image): on an external hard drive, DVDs or on a network.

ALL ABOUT APPS

INTRODUCTION TO APPS

One of the biggest changes that Windows 8.1 has brought to users is apps, something that was once the preserve of tablet and smartphone users.

WORKING WITH APPS

You'll find apps on tablets, smartphones, TVs and even the latest smartwatches. Therefore, it's inevitable that Window 8.1 will make the most of them too.

What Are Apps?

Apps are small programs that tend to do specific jobs and there's no one type of app. They are small, lightweight and often free, yet their simplicity makes them easy to use.

Above: A view of apps arranged helpfully on the Start screen

Where Do You Download Them?

In Windows 8.1, this is the Windows Store, which you can access from the Start screen.

The Default Apps

You'll meet apps as soon as you log in to Windows 8.1. The Start screen is home to a host of apps, like Email, Photos and People.

THE STOCK WINDOWS APPS EXPLAINED

Windows 8.1 is packed with a host of apps as soon as you turn on your PC for the first time. Here's what they do.

OneDrive

OneDrive is the key part of Windows 8.1's 'cloud' storage, and you get 7 GB of storage for documents and photos on the web.

Reading List

This app stores articles you enjoy online, and saves them to be read when you're away from an internet connection.

Skype

A video messaging app that will find existing contacts from your old contacts in Hotmail, MSN Messenger and other programs. When a contact is online, you'll see a green dot next to their profile. To start chatting, just tap the online contact.

Bing Weather

A weather app giving short-term and long-range forecasts, overlaid on gorgeous backgrounds.

Above: You can easily copy over any files, such as photos, to the cloud with OneDrive.

Bing News

You can swipe through the news like a giant newspaper and, when you click on a story, it's easy to read and clearly laid out.

Bing Sports

Sports fans are well catered for with this well-laid-out app. It's a great way to keep up with the news, and benefits from a breadth of sources.

Bing Travel

Packed with city guides and photos from over 2,000 destinations, Bing Travel is a fantastic app for those who love to travel.

Bing Finance

This finance app is on hand to give you live updates straight to the Windows 8.1 Start screen.

Hot Tip

The Bing Finance app also has a currency converter built in. Just access the options menu by swiping from the bottom or right-clicking. As it's connected to the web, all exchange rates will be current.

As well as general information on the FTSE and Dow Jones, you can watch your own portfolio too.

Bing Maps

You can navigate around the globe, get live traffic information and routes, and check out local hotels, shops and restaurants.

Above: From transport to accommodation, Bing Travel helps you find everything you need.

PHOTOS APP

The place for viewing photos on your Windows 8.1 PC, Photos also enables you to connect to OneDrive to see your photos too.

EDITING YOUR SNAPS

To make an edit, view the image full screen and then click or tap anywhere on your picture. There are quick options to rotate or crop your image at the bottom.

Advanced Editing

Bring up the options menu again by clicking on the photo and then press Edit in the bottom-right corner – the view will change to have more edits on the left, and previews on the right.

Hot Tip

If you want to improve your snaps without the hassle, then Autofix is your friend. Just make sure the option is selected on the left and then tap the panels on the right to check out possible changes.

Above: The Photos app offers various advanced editing options and previews of changes made.

Above: To adjust colour temperature, click the button and turn the dial in the required direction.

Basic Fixes

Tap this option and the right panel will change, and show the same rotate and crop options you'll recognize from the main screen. In addition, you'll see options for red-eye removal and retouch.

Light

This option lets you control the brightness, contrast, highlights and shadows in your photos.

Colour

This option enables you to change the temperature (how warm the colours are), add tints, change the saturation of the colours and enhance the colours in your photos.

Effects

The last two effects are two of the best in the Photo app: the ability to add a vignette and the addition of a focus point to your images.

PEOPLE APP

More than just your standard contacts app, the People app brings together everyone from your email and social networks into one place.

EXPLORING CONTACTS

You can search for specific contacts using the search bar in the top right, or browse using the A–Z tabs on the home screen.

GET UP TO DATE

The What's New tab enables you to get updates from their social networks so you can see everything in one place. A timeline of updates from your contacts will appear, with updates from Twitter, Facebook, LinkedIn, Outlook and more.

ADD SOCIAL MEDIA

It's a great contacts app as well, and you can search your contacts using the alphabetical tabs on the right and then choose how you'd like to contact them – by email, Skype, Twitter or Facebook.

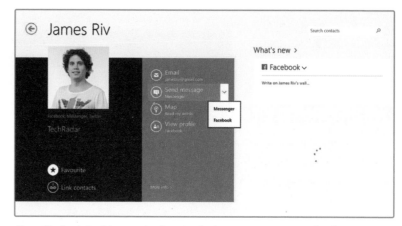

Above: The People App brings together the multitude of ways you can contact your friends and family in one place.

XBOX APPS

There are three Xbox apps that come as part of the Windows 8.1 package. Here, we give you an overview of what you can do with the Games, Music and Video apps.

XBOX GAMES

Windows 8.1 and the Xbox are built to work together, but even if you don't have a Microsoft console, there's still plenty on offer here. Games have become a huge part of the Windows 8.1 apps offering, and the Games app can track achievements and progress.

XBOX MUSIC

Streaming – the act of subscribing to a service and listening to any music you want over the internet – is a great way to enjoy music. For more on using Xbox Music, *see* page 94.

XBOX VIDEO

To rent and buy movies at the Xbox Video service, just tap or click the Video tile. *See* page 102 to find out how to get the most from it.

Above: The Xbox Games app enables you to edit gaming profiles and show achievements and much more.

MAIL APP

The Mail app has been given an overhaul in Windows 8.1. You can run multiple email accounts simultaneously, making it perfect for home and business users alike.

SET UP YOUR EMAIL

If you've signed in with your Windows ID, the Mail app will open with your email already present. Whichever email you've used for your Windows ID will be found as soon as you open the app.

Add Other Accounts

When you open the app, Windows should prompt you to add any other accounts. You can have as many as you like. If Windows doesn't prompt you, see below for what to do:

1. Open the Mail app from the Start screen.

2. Bring up the Charms bar and choose Settings.

3. Tap or click Accounts.

4. Tap or click Add an account, choose your type of account, then add your username and password.

Above: The Mail app is clearly laid out, with certain types of emails being handily filed away separately.

USING THE MAIL APP

Hot Tip

To add an email signature, open the Settings charm, tap or click Accounts, and choose the correct email account. Find the Use a signature option and write your sign-off.

○ **Reply**, **Reply All**, or **Forward**: Tap or click the Reply icon in the upper-right corner.

○ **Delete messages**: Select one or more messages and then tap or click the Trash icon.

○ **Search for messages**: Tap or click the Search icon or simply begin typing in the Mail app.

○ **Print a message**: Select an email message, then open the Devices charm, tap or click Print, choose a printer, then choose Print.

○ **Send attachments**: In a new email message, tap or click the paperclip icon. Select the file you want to add to the message and then tap or click Attach.

Above: To print an email, select Print in the Devices charm, choose a printer and settings (such as page orientation), then Print.

○ **Create folders and move messages**: Swipe down from the top of the screen. Tap or click Folder options to create a new folder, or tap or click Move to move the selected messages.

○ **Add a contact**: Tap or click an email address from an email to create a new entry in the People app. Tap or click the Save icon in the top-right corner.

CALENDAR APP

The Calendar app in Windows 8.1 is more limited than its Mail counterpart. However, it's still an excellent app with plenty of great options.

MASTER YOUR CALENDAR'S VIEWS

The Windows 8.1 Calendar app has a host of views which enable you to see your appointments, dates and events. You can switch between them by accessing the Options menu.

Add Appointments

Access the Options menu and choose New. In a new window you can add a title, date, time and location. You can also add notes and information.

Show More

Click or tap the Show more link for more options for your calendar entry. You can add attendees if they're in your People app. You can also set reminders, and the drop-down menu enables you to set an alarm before the start of an event.

Above: You can sync your Facebook or Outlook account to your Calendar in order to see contacts' birthdays.

DOWNLOAD APPS

As well as the apps that come as standard with Windows 8.1, there is a whole world of apps waiting for you to download in the Windows Store.

GET STARTED WITH THE WINDOWS STORE

All apps are found within the Windows Store, which is available on all Windows 8.1 devices. You can find the link on your Start screen, indicated by the shopping bag on the green tile.

Signing In

To download apps from the Windows Store, you need a Windows account, which you should have set up when logging into Windows for the first time. Enter your username and password at the first screen.

Above: Before downloading any new apps, you need to sign into the Windows Store.

Browsing The Store

You'll notice that the apps disappear at the right-hand side of the screen, and the page scrolls right through a list of app categories, including Social for networking apps, Entertainment for TV and movies, and of course Games.

Above: Search the Store by typing what you're looking for into the field in the top-right corner – results will appear as you type.

Searching The Store

The search box is located top-right, and it's easy to type what you're looking for. Just tap into the box, start typing and the results will appear as you type, narrowing with every stroke. When you see your app appear, just tap or click it to be taken to its page.

- ○ **Free apps:** The Windows Store has a category to let you browse free apps on the main page, and every category has its own free library too, so you can weed out the deals.

- ○ **Paid-for apps:** Paid-for apps are better quality than the free ones. You can see the paid-for ones on the home screen, and in each app category.

Hot Tip

Each category has a sub-section for new, top paid, top free, and a selection of sub-categories. Just tap or click any of these headings to get even more choice.

BUYING APPS

Before splashing out on an app, it's well worth checking that you're buying a quality product, so it's best to read the comments from other app users.

How To Download An App

Free apps will have an Install button, while paid-for ones will have Buy. To install an app, just tap the button and a notification will appear in the top right-hand corner to let you know that the app is installing.

- **Buying paid-for apps:** When you press Buy, you'll be asked to confirm your account's password before being whisked off to the payment page. You'll need to enter card details, which will be saved for next time.

Above: You don't have to enter payment details to download a free app, but it might be handy if you expect to buy apps.

HOW TO USE APPS

As you'd imagine with the customizable Windows 8.1, there are many ways to get more from apps, from organizing them to work more efficiently to multitasking.

MASTER YOUR APPS

Once you've downloaded your apps, getting the most out of them is key to your Windows 8.1 experience.

Find An App

To access an app just scroll through the Start screen. Tap or click any app tile or list item to open the app.

App Multitasking

You can run up to four apps on the screen at any one time. Just drag the top of your app – either with your finger or the mouse – to either side of the screen to snap it into place, then just load another and it will sit in the vacant space. You can resize it by dragging the black bar.

Above: You can organize and customize the Start screen to have your apps set up your way.

Switch Between Apps

Swipe in from the left-hand edge and you'll switch back to the last app you were using. Keyboard and mouse users should place the mouse pointer in the top-left corner for a preview of the app. Click to make it full screen.

Hot Tip

When you resize an app, the display will change to accommodate its new shape.

See All Apps

On a touch-screen device, swipe in from the left (as if switching apps), then slide back to the edge again; with a mouse, put the pointer in the top-left corner and then move it down the left-hand edge.

Close An App

Click or tap and hold at the top of the app screen and drag it down to the bottom.

Delete Your Apps

Tap and hold an app and the Options bar will appear at the bottom. Tap or click Uninstall.

Above: Switch between apps by swiping previous apps out from the left-hand edge.

ORGANIZE YOUR START SCREEN

Tidy up your Start screen by organizing your apps: try banishing rarely used icons or increasing an app's size.

Pin Apps To The Start Screen

1. On the Start screen, slide up from the middle of the screen to see the Apps view. (With a mouse, click the arrow button near the lower-left corner of the screen.)

2. Press and hold or right-click to select the apps you want to pin.

3. Tap or click Pin to Start.

Resize An App

Tap and hold to bring up the Options bar and choose Resize. Choose how much space the tile takes up on your Start screen.

Create A Group Of Tiles

On the Start screen, press and hold or right-click the tiles you want to group together. Drag them to an open space and when a grey bar appears behind them, release the tiles. Tap or click where it says Name group and enter a new name.

Above: Choose favourite apps to pin to your Start screen to make them even more accessible.

GETTING CONNECTED

INTRODUCTION TO THE WORLD WIDE WEB

Windows 8.1 is the most connected version of Microsoft's OS to date, so if you're ready to see all that it's capable of, it's time to connect to the world wide web.

WEB JARGON EXPLAINED

Let us translate some of the lingo for you.

Airplane Mode

When travelling on aircraft, you are only permitted to use tablets and laptops that are turned to Airplane Mode. In Windows 8.1, you can access this in PC Settings.

Browser

This is the program on your PC that enables you to view web pages and surf the web.

Cloud

The catch-all name given for services that live on the web. OneDrive, Dropbox and Hotmail are all examples of cloud services.

Download

Any information transferred from the internet and saved locally to your PC has been downloaded.

HomeGroup

This is the name for the managed network of Windows 8.1, Windows 8 and Windows 7 devices in the home, as well as devices such as printers.

IP Address

This is the unique long number that serves as your device's identity on your network and the internet in general.

ISP

This is your Internet Service Provider, the company that provides your connection to the web.

Malware

Any virus, spyware or small malicious app designed to do damage to your PC or steal information from you.

Mobile Broadband

Mobile broadband uses the 3G and 4G networks, predominantly used by mobile phones.

Modem

A modem is the gateway between your home network and the internet. Most routers supplied by ISPs have a modem built in.

Network

A network is the name for a collection of PCs, printers or other devices linked together.

Router

This is the device that distributes your internet connection to devices around the home.

Security Key

The password used for accessing a network. It's important to set up a password for your own Wi-Fi, so that people can't access it without your knowledge.

Spam

This is unsolicited email, which can often spread malware.

Proxy

This is another type of connection, where your location is hidden, or broadcast as somewhere else.

Upload

This is the process of information leaving your devices or network and being loaded on to the internet.

URL

This is the unique address for a website. The address www.bbc.co.uk is a URL.

Above: When you type a URL (uniform resource locator) into your browser, it will provide you with a link so you can connect straight through to a particular website.

WPA2

This is a type of Wi-Fi security. When setting up a network, look out for this option, which will make your home Wi-Fi more secure.

Wi-Fi/Wireless

Wireless, more commonly called Wi-Fi, is the method of connecting to a network without plugging in.

GET CONNECTED TO THE INTERNET

If you already have an internet connection set up, it's just a case of getting your new Windows 8.1 PC connected.

WHAT YOU NEED

- A subscription to an ISP's broadband service.
- A modem router.
- A PC that has a network adaptor (every modern PC will have this).
- A network (Ethernet) cable.

For Wireless Connectivity

- A wireless modem router (every modern router will have this).

- A PC with a wireless card (all laptops and tablets will have this, but check desktop PCs).

Above: To connect to a Wi-Fi network, go to Settings/Network, and choose from the networks listed there.

CONNECT VIA ETHERNET

After you've signed up to an ISP and you've connected your hardware by following the ISP's instructions, you should be ready to connect to the internet. Just plug an Ethernet cable into the back of the router and then into your Windows 8.1 PC.

CONNECT TO A WI-FI NETWORK

You can connect to a network by swiping in from the right edge of the screen, tapping Settings, then choosing Network. Click or tap the Wi-Fi option. Choose the network you want to connect to, then tap or click Connect. Enter the network security key and password and then click OK.

CONNECT VIA WPS (WI-FI PROTECTED SET-UP)

If your router has a WPS button, you can connect without the hassle of passwords and logins. Turn on the PC and once at the Windows Start screen, connect to a network by swiping in from the right edge of the screen, tapping Settings and going to PC Settings and choosing the network.

KEEP YOUR DATA PRIVATE

When using public Wi-Fi you should be vigilant and use the public network settings.

Public Network Protection

1. Swipe in from the right edge of the screen, then tap Settings. With a mouse, point to the bottom-right corner of the screen, move the pointer up, click Settings and choose PC Settings from the bottom right-hand corner.

2. Tap or click Network, then Connections, and find the name of the network you want to connect to.

3. Turn off Find devices and content. However, remember to switch it on again when you get home.

Above: Protect data: turn the Find devices and content setting off.

BROWSE THE WEB WITH INTERNET EXPLORER

Internet Explorer is the default browser in Windows 8.1, which is your gateway to surfing the web on your PC.

THE MODERN UI INTERNET EXPLORER

The touch-friendly version of Internet Explorer can be accessed using the tile on the Start screen, with the bar for entering web addresses appearing at the bottom.

Bookmark A Website

Swipe up from the bottom edge and choose the Favorites button. Tap the star icon next to the URL bar to access previously stored bookmarks.

InPrivate Browsing

If you don't want other PC users to see the sites you've been using, you can use the InPrivate feature. Swipe up from the bottom edge, choose the Tab tools button and then the New InPrivate tab.

Above: IE is Windows' default browser, available as both touch and non-touch versions.

Pin A Site To Your Start Screen

You can pin sites you use all the time as tiles to your Start screen. Swipe up from the bottom edge to bring up the app commands. Tap the Favorites button, then Pin site button and tap Pin to Start.

Save Pages To A Reading List

When you come across content that you'd like to read later, you can add it to a reading list. Access the Share charm and then choose Reading List to add it.

INTERNET EXPLORER 11 (DESKTOP)

The desktop version of Internet Explorer is more traditional, and much better suited to those using desktop PCs and large-screen laptops.

Above: Come back and browse it later by adding it to your Reading List

Change Default Search Provider

Click the settings cog on the taskbar and choose Internet Options followed by Manage.

Download Files

To download a file, just click the link on a web page. IE will ask you if you want to download it and will give you two options: 'Run' will download the file and open it straightaway, while 'Save' will add it to your downloads library or other specified location.

Use Add-ons

Add-ons are small apps that sit within Internet Explorer and help you get more done.
Go to the Manage add-ons menu and choose Find more toolbars and extensions at the
bottom of the menu.

Add Bookmarks

Click the star icon on the toolbar. The Favorites menu will pop up. Choose Add to favorites.

InPrivate Browsing

Head to the cog icon on the taskbar, choose Safety and then InPrivate browsing.

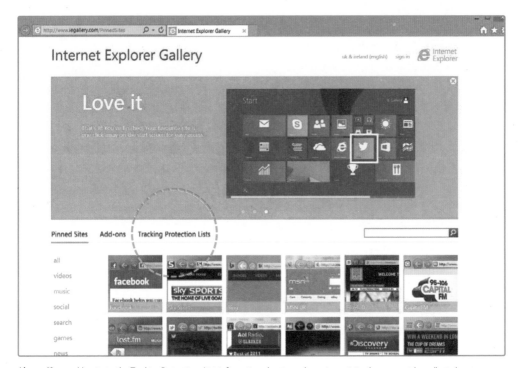

Above: If you add a site to the Tracking Protections List, information about your browsing activity there cannot be collected.

NETWORK YOUR PCS

Networking means linking your PCs together in your home so they act as one giant machine and you can share your data across all PCs.

WINDOWS HOMEGROUP

A HomeGroup is Windows 8.1's name for a group of PCs on a home network that can share files and printers. HomeGroup is available in Windows 8.1, Windows RT 8.1 and Windows 7.

Creating A HomeGroup

When you set up a PC with Windows 8.1 or Windows RT 8.1, a HomeGroup is created automatically on the first PC. However, if you clicked to disable sharing, you will need to re-enable it.

1.   Swipe in from the right edge of the screen, tap Settings, PC Settings, and then tap or click Network followed by HomeGroup.

2.   Tap or click Create. Select the libraries and devices that you want to share.

Adding Your Other PCs To The HomeGroup

1.   Find the HomeGroup password: swipe in from the right edge of the screen, tap Settings, PC Settings, and then tap or click Network followed by HomeGroup. The password will be displayed at the bottom of the screen.

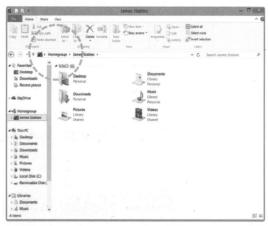

Above: Having a HomeGroup makes it easy to share files.

2. Go to the PC you want joined to the network, open the HomeGroup menu again, enter the HomeGroup password and then tap or click Join.

3. Enter the HomeGroup password, then tap or click Join.

4. Select the libraries and devices that you want this PC to have access to.

Finding HomeGroup Files

To access shared libraries on other HomeGroup PCs, open This PC by swiping in from the right edge of the screen, tapping Search and entering This PC in the search box and choosing this option from the list. Under HomeGroup, tap or click the libraries you want to access. You'll now see a list of files. Double-tap or double-click the files or folders you want.

Sharing Libraries

When you create or join a HomeGroup, you select the libraries and devices you want to share with other people in the HomeGroup. Libraries are initially shared with read-only access.

Share Individual Files

To share individual files or folders, search for 'This PC' on the Start screen and choose from the list. Select the item, then tap or click the Share tab.

Above: All files in the HomeGroup can be seen in File Explorer.

Above: To share a file, tap the Share tab and select a share option.

ADVANCED SHARING

Sharing in Windows 8.1 is almost unrivalled, but you won't want to share everything with everyone. Luckily, it's easy to change permissions as you go.

CHANGE PERMISSIONS

Access the advanced sharing option in Windows Explorer by clicking once on any file or folder and then clicking the Sharing tab on the toolbar.

The Permissions box lists everyone who has access to the file, and what level of control they have over it.

SHARING A PRINTER

1. Open HomeGroup by swiping in from the right edge of the screen.

2. Tap or click the control to Share printers and devices.

3. Once the printer has been shared, you will be able to see it on any PC in the HomeGroup.

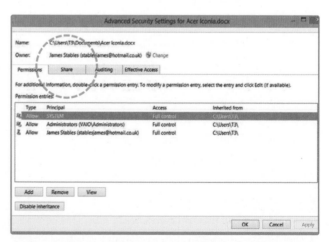

Above: The Permissions settings enable you to allow or deny specific users access to particular files or folders; to set this up, click the file or folder, then the Share tab.

CHANGE YOUR HOMEGROUP PASSWORD

The standard HomeGroup password is a random mix of numbers and letters, which can be hard to remember. The good news is that you can change your password to something a little more memorable. Here's how:

1. Head to the Control Panel by summoning the Settings charm while on the Windows 8.1 desktop.

2. Under the Network and Internet heading, click Choose HomeGroup and sharing options.

3. Tap or click Change HomeGroup password, then Settings menu, and choose Change PC Settings.

4. Tap or click Change the password. You might be asked for an admin password or to confirm your choice. Press OK when you're done.

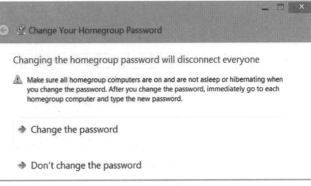

Above: Change your HomeGroup password to something memorable.

SET UP A NETWORK HARD DRIVE

If you have multiple PCs in your home, it's possible to back them all up to a single hard drive, called a network hard drive.

WHAT'S A NETWORK HARD DRIVE?

Network Attached Storage (NAS) means you have a hard drive accessed over your home network, rather than directly connected to your PC. Unlike your computer's hard drive, which is inside your PC, a NAS drive connects to your home router.

WHY NETWORK YOUR HARD DRIVE?

The advantages of a networked drive are numerous: it can be shared by any computer on your network and also makes for a fantastic backup – if a PC were to lose its data, the NAS drive would be unaffected.

Set Up Your Network Hard Drive

1. Connect your networked drive to your home router and install the installation software.

2. Type 'network' on the Start screen and find your drive in the list.

3. Right-click or tap and hold This PC in the left-hand pane and choose Map Network Drive.

4. Choose a letter for your networked drive and choose it from the list of networked items.

5. Your network drive can be accessed by any PC on your network, as long as the set-up process is repeated for each device.

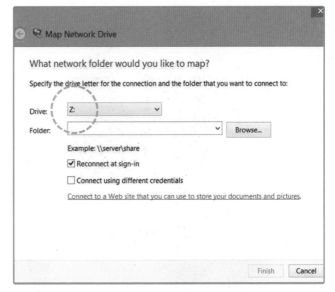

Above: When you map a network hard drive, you are creating a shortcut to it; during the setup process, you should assign it a letter.

USE THE CLOUD WITH ONEDRIVE

In Windows 8.1, you get a whopping 7 GB of storage in OneDrive, which is Microsoft's own 'cloud' or web-storage service.

WHAT CAN YOU DO WITH ONEDRIVE?

With OneDrive you can share any file easily from within Windows Explorer. To do this, just copy the file or folder you want to share to OneDrive.

Share Your Files

When you save your files to OneDrive, you can share them with other people by sending a link in an email, or post on sites like Facebook, Twitter or LinkedIn.

Add Files To OneDrive Using The App

On the Start screen, tap or click OneDrive. Access the Options menu by right-clicking or swiping up from the bottom. Tap or click folders to browse to the location on OneDrive to which you want to add the files.

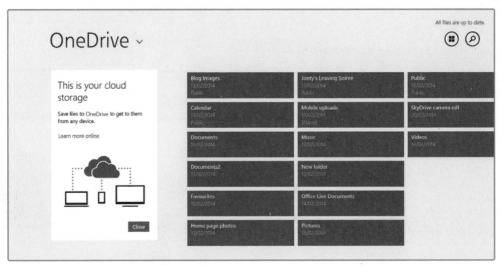

Above: Store 7 GB of data on OneDrive and access it from anywhere, as long as you're connected to the internet.

Save Files To Your PC

Just tap any file and it will open in a compatible program. If you right-click or swipe on a file and select Make available offline, that file will be copied to your hard drive.

Hot Tip

For photos, tap or click Camera roll and then choose Upload photos at good quality.

Automatically Saving Backup OneDrive

Swipe in from the right-hand edge of the screen, tap Settings, then tap Change PC Settings. For documents, tap or click OneDrive, and then switch on Save documents to OneDrive by default.

Access Microsoft Office Web Apps

OneDrive comes with web versions of all the Office apps, such as Word, Excel and PowerPoint. To access the Office web apps, you need to log in to OneDrive using the web. In your browser, go to onedrive.com and sign in with the same Microsoft ID you use for your Windows 8.1 PC.

MUSIC, VIDEO & PHOTOS

THE XBOX MUSIC APP

Your Windows PC is packed with ways to enjoy music, with not one but two dedicated apps for listening to your favourite tunes.

LISTENING TO MUSIC

On the Windows 8.1 Start screen is the all-new music app Xbox Music, which has over 30 million songs available online.

Streaming Music

The Xbox Music app needs a £8.99/$9.99 per month XBox Music Pass to activate, in return for which you get to listen to an unlimited number of songs in its catalogue.

GETTING STARTED WITH XBOX MUSIC

The top of the window has three buttons: Albums, Artists and Songs. Press one of these options and the music displayed on the screen will change to reflect that option.

Above: The XBox Music app allows you to stream music as well as manage your own.

Find Your Music

When the app is open, tap the three-lines icon in the top left to open the Xbox Music menu. Tap or click the Collection option and the main pane will change to display all your music.

Add Locations

If Xbox Music can't detect MP3s in the Music library, it will let you add a separate

Above: If you choose to search your music collection using the Artist option, the Xbox app will list all the songs or albums related to that artist.

Above: Music while you work? Entirely possible with Windows' app-snapping feature.

folder. Tap the option labelled 'we didn't find any music on this PC' and then choose the '+' icon. Browse to your folder of choice and press Add this folder to Music.

Play Your Music

Go to the Collection menu. Search for music using the Albums, Artists or Songs tabs. Select a song or album and then hit the Play button on the bottom bar.

Search For Music

Tap the search box and type the name of the artist, album or song you're looking for. The results will appear in the main window.

Multitask Your Music

To listen to music while using another app, use the snapping feature in Windows 8.1. Grab the top of the app and drag it to the left or right. When it snaps to half the screen, grab the three dots and resize the Xbox Music app to occupy a thin sliver at the far left or right of the screen.

CREATE A PLAYLIST IN XBOX MUSIC

You can group any bunch of songs together and create your perfect playlist.

1. In the left pane, choose New playlist, enter a name and then tap or click Save.

2. Now choose Collection, browse your songs, hit the '+' button and choose the playlist name from the left-hand pane.

To remove a song from a playlist, select it with a single click or tap and hit the '–' button when it appears.

3. Repeat until you have as many songs as you want.

4. When finished, find the playlist in the left pane and then tap or click the Play button.

START STREAMING IN XBOX MUSIC

Xbox Music offers a trial month free, so there's no reason not to dive into the world of music streaming.

1. Choose the Explore tab in the left-hand pane. At the top of the screen, tap the 'Get an Xbox Music Pass' link.

2. Tap the free-trial option and sign in using your Microsoft credentials.

3. Press the Add a credit card icon, enter your details and click Confirm.

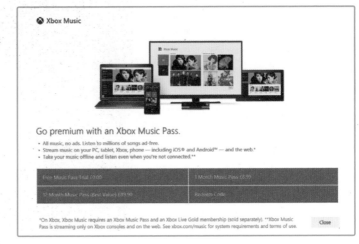

Above: Xbox Music lets you try before you buy (but only for 30 days).

WINDOWS MEDIA PLAYER

Windows Media Player is a powerful manager of offline music, and lets you listen to your MP3s, organize them, make playlists and much more besides.

INTRODUCING WINDOWS MEDIA PLAYER

Unlike the Xbox Music app, Windows Media Player lives on the desktop rather than on the Start screen.

Find Your Media In Windows Media Player

When you start Windows Media Player for the first time, it will scan your libraries for all media files. You can find them through the Music, Video and Pictures options in the left-hand pane.

RIP CDS TO YOUR PC

One of the best features of Windows Media Player is its ability to turn your CDs into digital music files and store them on your PC.

1. Make sure you're connected to the internet if you want Windows Media Player to get info about the songs automatically.

Above: The multitasking Windows Media Player is found on your desktop.

2. Open Windows Media Player.

3. Insert an audio CD into the PC's CD drive.

4. Tap or click the Rip CD button.

Change The Rip Settings
To access the settings menu, just click the Organize tab and then click Options. Click the Rip Music tab.

Choose The File Format
The default file format for ripping CDs in Windows Media Player is Windows Media Audio (WMA), but that's not the best option. Click the drop-down menu and change this option to MP3.

Change The Quality
Using the slider at the bottom of the window, you can up the quality from 128 kbps to 192 kbps.

Add Album Art Manually
If you find yourself with unidentified albums, Windows Media Player can help. Open Windows Media Player and go to the library window. Right-click any album that hasn't been identified and choose Find

Hot Tip
The top option in the Rip Music options menu is the location in which music is sent when you start ripping. The default location is the Music library in Windows 8.1, but if you want to have files stored in a different place, just choose Change.

Above: Use the options to alter your Rip settings.

album info. To force the player to update the file, click Organize and then click Apply media information changes.

SYNC MUSIC WITH A MOBILE DEVICE

You can use Windows Media Player to copy music, videos and photos from your Windows 8.1 device's library to a portable device, such as a smartphone, tablet or MP3 player.

Hot Tip

To watch a DVD using Windows Media Player, head to http://www.videolan.org and download the free VLC player.

Above: Sync Windows Media Player with your smartphone or tablet to make sure your entertainment is with you when you want it.

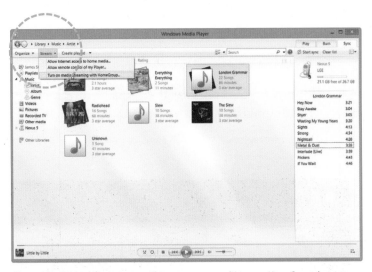

Above: The Stream tab's options enable you to stream media to your HomeGroup devices.

Start Syncing

Connect your chosen device to your PC and switch it on. Open Windows Media Player, then either tap or click Finish to sync automatically, or tap or click Finish, then tap or click the Sync tab to choose files manually.

STREAM TO OTHER DEVICES

You can also use Windows Media Player to stream content from your Windows 8.1 PC to other devices around the home, like a movie to a SmartTV.

Start Streaming

1. Open Windows Media Player and go to the library window.

2. Click the Stream tab on the toolbar and choose Turn on media streaming with HomeGroup.

3. A box will list all the devices in your home. Tick the Allowed box next to the devices you want to stream to, or hit the Allow All button, and press Next.

4. Make your selection by choosing Shared or Not Shared from the drop-down lists, and press Next. Make a note of the password and press Finish.

XBOX VIDEO

Like the Xbox Music app, Windows 8.1 comes with an app for video. It's designed for a touch screen, and you'll find it on your Start screen.

WATCH MOVIES ON YOUR PC

You can use the Video app to watch all of the video content already on your PC. Just follow these steps:

Above: Discover visual treats galore with the Xbox Video app.

1. Open the Xbox Video app.

2. Slide or scroll to the left to see your personal videos.

3. Tap or click a video to play it.

RENT MOVIES USING XBOX VIDEO

The main feature of the Xbox Video app is the huge library of films to rent and buy.

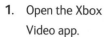
Hot Tip

You can quickly open any video file by swiping up from the bottom, or by right-clicking and choosing Open file.

Above: If you have enabled your other devices to stream using HomeGroup, then it's easy to watch your movie on your TV or Xbox 360.

1. To start watching videos, open up the Xbox Video app and you'll see a host of titles. Tapping a tile brings up options to watch your movie.

2. You can then buy the item outright or choose to rent it.

PLAY TO DEVICES USING XBOX VIDEO

In the same way that Windows Media Player can enable other devices to access its content, the Xbox Video app can do the same, and with an amazing twist.

To send a video to another device, start playing it as normal on your Windows 8.1 PC. Pause it immediately and then swipe in from the right, or place your mouse in the bottom right-hand corner to show the Charms bar and choose Devices. You can take a shortcut by pressing the Windows key + K.

ENJOY PHOTOS IN WINDOWS 8.1

Windows 8.1 is a fantastic way to enjoy your pictures and home videos. Keeping on top of this digital deluge can be difficult, but Windows 8.1 can stop you getting overwhelmed, while improving your photos to enjoy in the future.

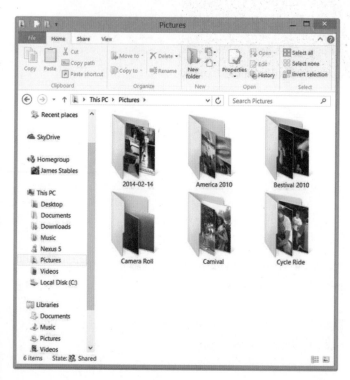

Above: The Pictures library is the go-to place for your snaps.

THE PICTURES LIBRARY

The default place for photos in Windows is the Pictures library, which you can access from File Explorer.

View Your Photos

Photos are displayed in the Photos app or Photo Viewer on the desktop. The real power is in the Photos app: photos are displayed in full screen, where you can edit your snaps, start slideshows or share them with friends.

Organize Photos

The best way to keep snaps organized is to put them in clearly named folders in the Pictures library. The Photos app will then use these names to create an album of your memories, which you can swipe or click through.

IMPORT PHOTOS

1. Connect your camera, smartphone or tablet to your PC using the USB cable and open the Photos app from the Start screen.

2. Swipe in from the bottom edge to see the application commands, or if you're using a mouse and keyboard, just right-click anywhere inside the main screen, and tap or click Import. Windows 8.1 will scan your camera and show all of your snaps in a long list with a small preview.

3. Tap or click the device you want to import from and then swipe or click each photo and video you want to import from the list.

4. Tap or click Import to have them copied to your Pictures library.

Nexus 5

Scanning your device. Files found: 57

Above: Once you've connected your device, the Photos app will scan it for photo files.

SHARING PHOTOS USING THE CHARMS BAR

1. To start sharing, open the Photos app. Go to the folder containing the photos you want to share. Access the Charms bar and choose Share. The app you're using to share, be it Facebook or Twitter, will be listed.

2. Choose the app you want to use from the list, and it will open inside the Photos app, taking up the right-hand side of the screen. Use the service as normal.

Hot Tip

Before you can start sharing with your favourite social media service, you need to download it as an app from the Windows Store and make sure you're logged in. Once that's done, you'll find it in the Share charm list.

UPLOAD PHOTOS TO ONEDRIVE

The OneDrive service, which provides Windows 8.1's cloud storage, is a great way to back up your photos. Because your OneDrive folders are baked into Windows 8.1 like any other hard drive, you can store your photos online. Find the folder within OneDrive, right-click and choose Include in library, followed by the Pictures option.

Make OneDrive A Pictures Library
Because your OneDrive folders are baked into

Above: Share great memories with friends via Charms, or through social media.

Windows 8.1 like any other hard drive, you can store your photos online, and use them just like any other library. Find the folder within OneDrive, right-click and choose Include in library followed by the Pictures option. It will now behave exactly as the traditional method, but instead of being on your PC's hard drive, it's safely stored in the cloud.

Hot Tip

If you import from a camera that contains images you've already copied to your PC, they will still appear in the list, but Windows 8.1 will detect them and they won't automatically be selected, to prevent duplication.

Above: Save your photos in OneDrive's cloud and they will be secure.

TROUBLESHOOTING & MAINTENANCE

KEEP WINDOWS 8.1 RUNNING SMOOTHLY

Your Windows PC needs regular maintenance. Luckily, the system is full of fantastic tools ensuring things keep running smoothly.

OPTIMIZE YOUR DRIVES

Performance can suffer over time, and you may experience a gradual reduction in performance unless your PC is well maintained. The main offender is your hard drive.

Disk Defragmenting

Disk defragmenting tidies up all your data, and puts it back together. Windows 8.1 has a built-in tool for defragging your drive. By default, it's set to run every week, but you can do it manually:

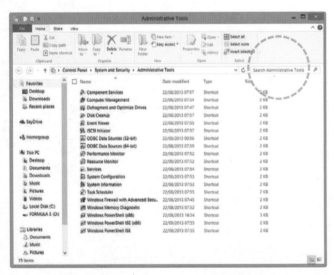

Above: You'll find the defragging program in Administrative Tools.

1. Open Optimize Drives by searching 'admin' on the Start screen, and then tapping or clicking Administrative Tools. Choose Defragment and Optimize Drives. Under Status, tap or click the drive you want to optimize. To help you determine if the drive needs to be optimized, tap or click Analyze.

2. Check the Current status column: if the drive is more than 10 per cent fragmented, you should optimize the drive now. Tap or click Optimize to start the process.

DISK CLEANUP

This is a great tool for de-cluttering your operating system, which has the benefit of making your PC run more quickly and saving hard drive space.

1. Search Administrative Tools and then double-tap or double-click Disk Cleanup. In the Drives list, tap or click the drive that you want to clean up, then tap or click OK.

2. You'll now see a host of checkboxes for the types of clutter that can be deleted. Tick as many as you want to delete. Press OK.

3. If you really want to save space, you can opt to clean up system files. This will include a host of Windows background information, which is not essential for Windows 8.1's day-to-day running.

Hot Tip

You can have your drives optimized automatically to make sure they are always in top condition. To do this, open the Optimize Drives window and check that scheduled optimization reads 'on'.

Above: Choose which items you want to delete for disk cleanup.

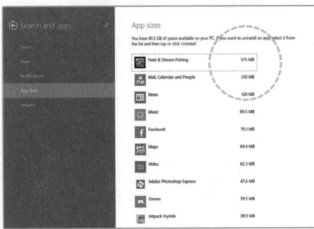

Above: You can easily see how much disk space is used by your apps.

KEEP ON TOP OF WINDOWS APPS

Windows 8.1 Start screen apps won't appear in the desktop cleanup options, but you can still get a summary of how much room they're taking up. Search for 'uninstall apps' on the Start screen, and choose Uninstall apps to free up disk space. Tap any app and hit Uninstall to delete it from your PC.

SPEED UP YOUR PC WITH POWER PLANS

Windows 8.1's power plans are profiles that tell the system how intensively to work. If your system is using the highest power it will run at its fastest rate, but this will have a negative effect on battery life.

What Power Plans Are Available?

- **Balanced**: Offers full performance when you need it and saves power when you don't. This is the best power plan for most people.

- **Power saver**: Saves power by reducing PC performance and screen brightness. If you're using a laptop, this plan can help you get the most from a single battery charge.

- **High performance**: Maximizes screen brightness and might increase PC performance. This plan uses a lot more energy.

Changing Power Plans

- **Laptop user**: If you use a laptop, it's really simple to switch plans. Just click the battery icon in the notification area at the far right of the taskbar. You will see two plans – Balanced or Power saver.

- **Non-laptop user**: If you aren't using a laptop, search for 'power options' on the Start screen and choose it from the list. Select the power plan you'd like to use, or tap or click Show additional plans.

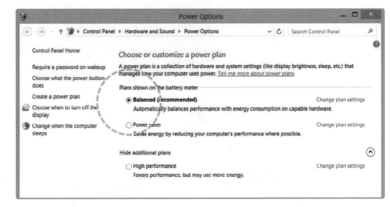

Above: Balanced is the best all-round power plan to use.

FIX WINDOWS PROBLEMS

While Windows 8.1 is the most advanced version of Microsoft's operating system, things can still go wrong from time to time.

RESET YOUR PC

Over time, the back end of Windows can get messy. In Windows 8.1, the ability to reset your PC has been built in, so if you find your PC crawling to a halt, you can press a button and have everything reset, without the difficult set-up. What's more, there's even an option to reset all the system files but keep your own files and settings intact. Here's how:

Above: Resetting your PC is the only way back to a genuinely clean, shop-fresh system, which hopefully runs faster. As the function is now built in to the system, it's much easier than reinstalling from a disk.

Perform A Partial Reset

You can solve PC problems such as slow performance by heading to the PC Settings menu, accessible via the Charms bar. Choose Update and recovery and, when the left-hand pane changes, choose Recovery.

Complete A Full Reset

This should be a final resort as a full reset will delete every file and setting on your PC, and return it to the same state as the day you bought it. Just press Get started.

Hot Tip

If you're not sure which System Restore point to pick, just pick the last date on which you're sure your system was working properly.

USE SYSTEM RESTORE

System Restore is a feature in Windows 8.1 that enables you to turn back time on your system, and have a top-running system resurrected on your PC. In the background, Windows 8.1 takes snapshots of your system in case things go wrong.

Revert To A Restore Point

Head to the Recovery menu in the Settings charm. Under Advanced Startup, tap or click Restart Now. Choose Troubleshoot and then Reset your PC, followed by Advanced options. The System Restore button will be on the following menu and you'll be asked to enter your password.

Follow the steps until you reach a list of points to which it can be restored. Each will have a description and a date. If you know the event that caused your issues, then choose the one before. Press Next, and your system will be restored and your PC will restart.

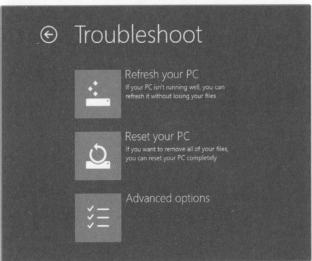

Above: Use the Advanced options under Advanced Startup to get to a list of restore points that your PC can be reverted to.

SOLVE STARTUP ISSUES

A PC that fails to start gives the user very little to work with, but follow these steps and you can overcome startup issues in no time.

WINDOWS 8.1 WON'T START

If your PC won't boot up at all, the troubleshooting tools can help you to roll back your PC to the last good configuration, or access Windows 8.1 in safe mode.

Log In Using Safe Mode

If Windows has detected a problem that's caused a boot failure, it should load up the diagnostic tools automatically. You can then choose Troubleshoot and then Safe Mode to log in to your account.

WINDOWS STARTUP TOOLS EXPLAINED

Startup Repair Tool

Once you've got Windows 8.1's troubleshooting menu to load, there is a variety of tools that can solve a PC that's not booting or not starting correctly.

Above: Safe Mode is a way of accessing Windows in a limited fashion, in order to diagnose the problem that is causing Windows to malfunction.

1. To access them, tap or click the Advanced options and choose Startup repair.

2. Tap or click the option in the troubleshooting list, and Windows 8.1 will go into a diagnostic mode.

3. Select the Windows account that's not booting and you'll be asked for your login information. Windows will then look for issues with your PC and attempt to fix any problems to get you into Windows.

Startup Settings

Press a number to choose from the options below.

Use number keys or function keys F1-F9.

1) Enable debugging
2) Enable boot logging
3) Enable low-resolution video
4) Enable Safe Mode
5) Enable Safe Mode with Networking
6) Enable Safe Mode with Command Prompt
7) Disable driver signature enforcement
8) Disable early launch anti-malware protection
9) Disable automatic restart after failure

Press F10 for more options
Press Enter to return to your operating system

Above: Startup Settings lists troubleshooting modes.

STARTUP SETTINGS

Windows 8.1 enables you to change a host of settings that can lead to common startup faults.

1. Choose Startup Settings from the list and at the next menu, tap or click Restart.

2. A list of numbered options will appear, and you just need to choose the correct one, pressing the corresponding number on your computer's keyboard.

FIX A SLOW PC

If you find your PC is slowing down, don't reach for the reset button quite yet. Aside from basic maintenance tasks, there are a few more ways to speed up a slouching system.

BASIC MAINTENANCE

If your PC is running slowly, check off these options first before taking further action.

Disk Cleanup

Unnecessary files can slow down your PC, so use Windows 8.1's built-in Disk Cleanup tool to get rid of computer clutter. Head to pages 111–112 for a full guide to using the Disk Cleanup feature.

Check For Malware And Viruses

A slow PC can be caused by malware. Windows Defender is our friend here. Search for it on the Start screen and run a full scan.

Check Memory Usage

If your PC is performing badly, press Ctrl + Alt + Delete and choose Task Manager from the list. Tap or click More details at the

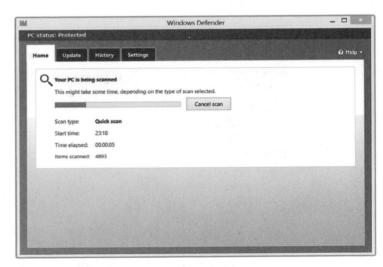

Above: Use Windows Defender to run a full scan to check for virus or spyware infections.

bottom, and you'll see a full list of running processes. Check out the levels of CPU, Memory and Disk it's using. If non-essential programs are eating up your resources, you can tap or click them and choose End task.

Above: In Programs and features, you can choose to delete items to free space.

Delete Programs

Search 'programs' on the Start screen and choose Programs and features from the list. You will see a list of your programs and their impact on your hard drive. Choose any program you want to remove and click Uninstall to banish it forever.

SPEED UP YOUR START

Windows 8.1's boot times are a dramatic improvement on previous versions of the operating system, but after a while, it can take a long time for your PC to become responsive when loading up.

Disable Apps From Starting With Windows

1. Press Ctrl + Alt + Delete and choose Task Manager.

2. Choose the Startup tab and a list of all the programs and services set to start with Windows will appear, and their impact on the time your PC takes to start will be shown as 'low', 'medium' or 'high'.

3. Many of these items will be non-essential, so click or tap them before hitting Disable. Remember, programs can be pinned to the taskbar or Start screen, so they can be launched easily without affecting your boot time.

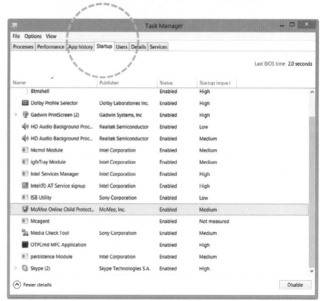

Above: If you don't need an application to open on startup, you can disable it in the Startup pane of Task Manager and it may speed up boot time.

FIX A PC THAT CRASHES

If your PC is crashing, or programs regularly stop responding, there can be many causes. Luckily, Windows 8.1 is full of tools that can help you get to the bottom of crashes.

DEAL WITH CRASHES

If a program crashes or becomes unresponsive, you need to bring up the Task Manager by pressing Ctrl + Alt + Delete. Choose Task Manager and the program that's failed from the list. If it has crashed, it should say 'not responding' next to it. Choose it from the list and tap or click End task to close it.

Check Windows 8.1 Event Viewer

If your PC is suffering from regular crashes, checking the built-in Event Viewer can reveal more information about what's causing errors. Events are classified either as an error, a warning or information.

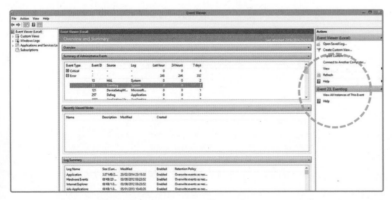

Just look for the error message associated with the time your computer froze or restarted. The error codes listed in the Event Viewer can be searched online, and it might mean the difference between fixing your PC at home and seeking expensive professional help.

Above: The Event Viewer allows you to view event logs on significant system events, to help pinpoint the causes of problems.

Above: Reduce display brightness to save battery power – do this via your keyboard, monitor buttons or the Settings charm.

GET LONGER BATTERY LIFE

The hugely increased power of a Windows 8.1 laptop or tablet means that all-day usage isn't easily achieved. However, with a few insider tips and tricks, you should be able to extend your usage.

○ **Use power plans:** You can switch to this by tapping or clicking the battery icon on the taskbar. *See* page 113.

○ **Reduce display brightness:** One of the biggest battery-draining offenders is your PC's display. Using your keyboard's function keys to turn down the brightness can help.

○ **Disconnect:** Turning off or unplugging devices that you aren't using will help to save battery. Also, take out CDs from your drives.

FIXING OTHER PROBLEMS

Before resorting to spending hours on the phone to tech support, or throwing your PC out of the window in frustration, read on.

DEVICE MANAGER

You can see every device on your system in the Device Manager option. Just search for 'hardware' on the Start screen, choose the System option and click or tap the Device Manager option in the top-left. Here, you can locate any piece of hardware, whether it's inside your PC or a peripheral like a printer or scanner. If there's a problem, a yellow warning sign will show.

FIX PRINT PROBLEMS

Check that the power supply to the printer is on and the printer cable is properly connected. If printing wirelessly, make sure that the printer's wireless option is switched on and available. If both of these are fine and the printer is still not working, you may need to take further action, such as installing new or updated drivers (these are the small pieces of software that act as go-betweens for your Windows PC and the printer). While any updating should be done automatically, here's how to find new drivers for your printer.

1. Go to the Settings charm, choose Update and recovery and then Windows Update. Check for updates with your printer connected, and restart your PC afterwards.

Hot Tip

The internet is full of forums that can help you with more obscure problems. Good support forums include www.eightforums.com and www.tomshardware.co.uk/forum/. Googling the problem is often the best way to find a solution.

2. Install software from the printer manufacturer. If your printer came with a disc, this is the best place to look.

3. Download and install the updated driver yourself. You can search for the correct driver software on the manufacturer's website.

Above: Windows help topics are accessed online; just go to Settings and select Help, and you will be taken there.

Adding More RAM

A simple and cheap upgrade to your PC; the only problem is buying the right type. You can use the tool at www.crucial.com to find out the type you need for your PC or laptop. Upgrading your RAM can improve a sluggish PC, which has problems when running lots of apps simultaneously.

Replacing Laptop Battery

Most laptops will have a removable battery, which can be removed by unclipping the catches underneath your machine. However, every battery is different, and you will need to buy the exact type for your laptop model.

Check Windows Update

Try running an update by going to the Settings charm and then Update and recovery followed by Windows Update. This will look for drivers for your sound card, which may fix the problem.

MORE WAYS TO GET HELP

No simple guide to Windows can cover every eventuality and problem, but if you can't fix a problem from these pages, there are plenty of ways to get help.

USEFUL WEBSITES AND FURTHER READING

WEBSITES

www.askvg.com/
Tips, tweaks, troubleshooting and customization for Windows.

www.computerhope.com/cleaning.htm
Lots of tips on how to give your PC a spring clean.

www.facebook.com/windowsmag
Facebook version of the Windows Magazine.

www.howtogeek.com/
Discussion, articles and reviews on all things PC related.

www.itpro.co.uk/desktop-software
News and insight from the IT business.

www.nidirect.gov.uk/choosing-a-computer
Straightforward advice on the best type of computer to choose for your needs.

www.pcadvisor.co.uk
Great advice on all things PC: device reviews, articles, forums and more.

www.recyclenow.com
If you are upgrading your computer or hardware, this site will tell you how to recycle it.

strongpasswordgenerator.com
Need a new password? This site will help you choose a good one.

www.techspot.com
A great, general interest site for everything to do with PCs.

which.co.uk/technology/computing
Unbiased advice on buying the computer and related technology that suits you best.

windowsforum.com/
A useful forum which contains information on how to deal with many common issues and questions about Windows.

windows.microsoft.com/en-gb/windows/support
Go to this site for help and information on anything Windows related.

winsupersite.com/
A great site covering all things Windows related.

FURTHER READING

Ballew, Joli, *Configuring Windows 8.1*, Microsoft Press, 2014

Bott, Ed, *Introducing Windows 8.1 for IT Professionals*, Microsoft Press, 2013

Boyce, Jim et al., *Windows 8.1 Bible*, John Wiley & Sons, 2014

McFedries, Paul, *PCs for Grown-ups: Getting the Most Out of Your Windows 8 Computer*, QUE, 2013

Miller, Michael, *Computer Basics Absolute Beginner's Guide, Windows 8.1 Edition*, QUE, 2014

Northrup, Tony, *Windows 8.1 Inside Out*, Microsoft Press, 2013

Price, Michael, *Windows 8 for Seniors*, In Easy Steps, 2012

Rathbone, Andy, *Windows 8.1 for Dummies*, John Wiley & Sons, 2013

Sievers, Tim, *Top 100 Tips for Windows 8: Discover the Secrets of Windows 8*, CreateSpace Independent Publishing Platform, 2012

Smith, Stephie, *BASICS of Windows: The Easy Guide to Your PC*, CreateSpace Independent Publishing Platform, 2013

Williams, Andy, *Migrating to Windows 8: For computer users without a touch screen, coming from XP, Vista or Windows 7*, CreateSpace Independent Publishing Platform, 2013

Yarnold, Stuart, *Windows 8 Tips, Tricks & Shortcuts*, In Easy Steps, 2012

INDEX